OTHER BOOKS BY JEFF KINNEY

Diary of a Wimpy Kid

Diary of a Wimpy Kid: Rodrick Rules

Coming soon:

Diary of a Wimpy Kid: The Last Straw

DIARY
of a Wimpy Kid
Do-It-Yourself Book

by Jeff Kinney

YOUR
PICTURE
HERE
↓

AMULET BOOKS
New York

The Library of Congress has catalogued the hardcover edition of this book under the following Control Number: 2008927175

ISBN: 978-0-8109-7149-3

Printed and bound in U.S.A.
10 9 8 7 6 5 4

HNA ■■■■■
harry n. abrams, inc.
a subsidiary of La Martinière Groupe
115 West 18th Street
New York, NY 10011
www.hnabooks.com

THIS BOOK BELONGS TO:

_____

IF FOUND, PLEASE RETURN
TO THIS ADDRESS:

_____

_____

(NO REWARD)

What're you gonna do with this thing?

OK, this is your book now, so technically you can do whatever you want with it.

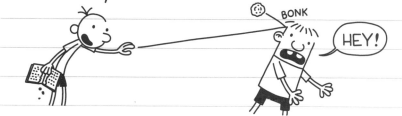

But if you write anything in this journal, make sure you hold on to it. Because one day you're gonna want to show people what you were like back when you were a kid.

Whatever you do, just make sure you don't write down your "feelings" in here. Because one thing's for sure: This is NOT a diary.

Your DESERT

If you were gonna be marooned for the rest of your life, what would you want to have with you?

Video games
1. Black ops
2. football
3.

Songs
1.
2.
3.

THIS STINKS.

ISLAND picks

Books

1.
2.
3.

Movies

1.
2.
3.

Have you

Have you ever gotten a haircut that was so bad you needed to stay home from school?

YES ☑ NO ☐

Have you ever had to put suntan lotion on a grown-up?

YES ☑ NO ☐

Have you ever been bitten by an animal?

YES ☑
NO ☐

Have you ever been bitten by a person?

YES ☑
NO ☐

Have you ever tried to blow a bubble with a mouthful of raisins?

YES ☐ NO ☑

EVER...

Have you ever peed in a swimming pool?

YES ☐   NO ☑

Have you ever been kissed full on the lips by a relative who's older than seventy?

YES ☑   NO ☐

Have you ever been sent home early by one of your friends' parents?

YES ☐   NO ☑

Have you ever had to change a diaper?

A LITTLE HELP?

YES ☐   NO ☑

PERSONALITY

What's your favorite ANIMAL?

Dogs

Write down FOUR ADJECTIVES that describe why you like that animal:

(EXAMPLE: FRIENDLY, COOL, ETC.)

playful   exited

Funny   stuped

What's your favorite COLOR?

Blue

Write down FOUR ADJECTIVES that describe why you like that color:

My carpet   cool

my eyes   not Goth

The adjectives you wrote down for your favorite ANIMAL describe HOW YOU THINK OF YOURSELF.
The adjectives you wrote down for your favorite COLOR describe HOW OTHER PEOPLE THINK OF YOU.

TEST

ANSWER THESE QUESTIONS AND THEN FLIP THE BOOK UPSIDE DOWN TO FIND OUT THINGS YOU NEVER KNEW ABOUT YOURSELF.

What's the title of the last BOOK you read?

Direy oF wiby Kid

List FOUR ADJECTIVES that describe what you thought of that book:

Fnnny   Stuped

exiting   hnlareus

What's the name of your favorite MOVIE?

horr movies

Write down FOUR ADJECTIVES that describe why you liked that movie:

Scary   I

bloody

- -

The adjectives you wrote down for the last BOOK you read describe HOW YOU THINK OF SCHOOL.

The adjectives you wrote down for your favorite MOVIE describe WHAT YOU'LL BE LIKE in thirty years.

Unfinished

Zoo-Wee Mama!

COMICS

Zoo-Wee Mama!

Make your

OWN comics

Predict the

I TOTALLY CALLED IT!

AW, RATS!

I officially predict that twenty years from now cars will run on __water__ instead of gasoline. A cheeseburger will cost $__50__, and a ticket to the movies will cost $__70__. Pets will have their own __coats__s. Underwear will be made out of __cloth__. __nuthing__ will no longer exist. A __itite__ named __G.W. Bush__ _____ will be president. There will be more __cats__ than people.

The annoying catchphrase will be:
__Tricker treat smell__
__my feat give me somthing__
__good to eat__

WUBBA DUBB, MY TUBB?

RAT-A-TAT-TAT AND CHICKEN FAT!

FUTURE

Aliens will visit our planet in the year <u>2020</u> and make the following announcement:

<u>We will kill you</u>
<u>We will eat you</u>
<u>We will poop you</u>

BROCCOLI WAS NEVER MEANT TO BE EATEN!

I KNEW IT!

The number-one thing that will get on old people's nerves twenty years from now will be:

<u>tolk back</u>

<u>Mning</u>

CURSE THOSE FANCY JIMJAMS!

WHIRRRR

Predict the

IN FIFTY YEARS:

Robots and mankind will be locked in a battle for supremacy.　TRUE ☑　FALSE ☐

Parents will be banned from dancing within twenty feet of their children.　TRUE ☑　FALSE ☐

People will have instant-messaging chips implanted in their brains.　TRUE ☑　FALSE ☐

FUTURE

YOUR FIVE BOLD PREDICTIONS FOR THE FUTURE:

1. Flying cars

2. Caputriezed phone

3.

4.

5.

(WRITE EVERYTHING DOWN NOW
SO YOU CAN TELL YOUR FRIENDS
"I TOLD YOU SO" LATER ON.)

Predict YOUR

What you're basically gonna do here is roll a die over and over, crossing off items when you land on them, like this:

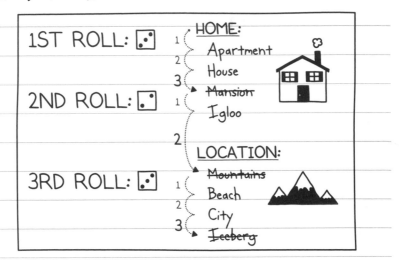

1ST ROLL: [die showing 3]

HOME:
1 Apartment
2 House
3 ~~Mansion~~
  Igloo

2ND ROLL: [die showing 2]

LOCATION:
1 ~~Mountains~~
2 Beach
3 City
  ~~Iceberg~~

3RD ROLL: [die showing 5]

Keep going through the list, and when you get to the end, jump back to the beginning. When there's only one item left in a category, circle it. Once you've got an item in each category circled, you'll know your future! Good luck!

MY LIFE STINKS.

future

HOME:
Apartment
House
Mansion
Igloo

LOCATION:
Mountains
Beach
City
Iceberg

KIDS:
None
One
Two
Ten

PET:
Dog
Cat
Bird
Turtle

JOB:
Doctor
Actor
Clown
Mechanic
Lawyer
Pilot
Pro athlete
Dentist
Magician
Whatever you want

VEHICLE:
Car
Motorcycle
Helicopter
Skateboard

SALARY:
$100 a year
$100,000 a year
$1 million a year
$100 million a year

Design your

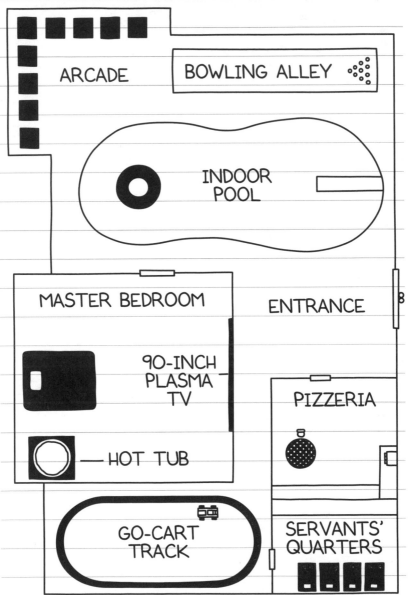

ARCADE

BOWLING ALLEY

INDOOR POOL

MASTER BEDROOM

ENTRANCE

90-INCH PLASMA TV

HOT TUB

PIZZERIA

GO-CART TRACK

SERVANTS' QUARTERS

DREAM HOUSE

YOUR FUTURE HOUSE

A few questions

What's the most embarrassing thing that ever happened to someone who wasn't you?

What's the worst thing you ever ate?

Vechibles

How many steps does it take you to jump into bed after you turn off the light?

5

How much would you be willing to pay for an extra hour of sleep in the morning?

$10

from GREG

Have you ever pretended you were sick so you could stay home from school?

No

(NEW VIDEO GAME)

Does it get on your nerves when people skip?

Did you ever do something bad that you never got busted for?

Unfinished

Ugly Eugene

COMICS

Ugly Eugene

Make your

OWN comics

Good advice to:

1. Don't use the bathroom on the second floor, because there aren't any stall doors in there.

2. Be careful who you sit next to in the cafeteria.

3. Don't pick your nose right before you get your school picture taken.

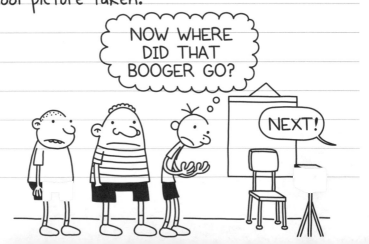

next year's class

1.

2.

3.

4.

Draw your FAMILY

the way Greg Heffley would

Your FAVORITES

TV show:

Band:

Sports team:

Food:

Celebrity:

Smell:

Villain:

Shoe brand:

Store:

Soda:

Cereal:

Super hero:

Candy:

Restaurant:

Athlete:

Game system:

Comic strip:

Magazine:

Car:

Your I EAST favorites

TV show:

Band:

Sports team:

Food:

Celebrity:

Smell:

Villain:

Shoe brand:

Store:

Soda:

Cereal:

Super hero:

Candy:

Restaurant:

Athlete:

Game system:

Comic strip:

Magazine:

Car:

Things you should do

☐ Stay up all night.

☐ Ride on a roller coaster with a loop in it.

☐ Get in a food fight. THWAP

☐ Get an autograph from a famous person.

☐ Get a hole in one in miniature golf.

☐ Give yourself a haircut.

☐ Write down an idea for an invention.

☐ Spend three nights in a row away from home.

☐ Mail someone a letter with a real stamp and everything.

Dear Gramma, Please send money.

I ONLY HAVE A FEW MORE TO GO!

before you get old

☑ Go on a campout.

ZZZ

☑ Read a whole book with no pictures in it.

?

☐ Beat someone who's older than you in a footrace.

☐ Make it through a whole lollipop without biting it.

☐ Use a porta-potty.

KNOCK KNOCK

OCCUPIED!

☐ Score at least one point in an organized sport.

☐ Try out for a talent show.

EH?

Five things NOBODY KNOWS about you

BECAUSE THEY NEVER BOTHERED TO ASK

1.

2.

3.

4.

5.

I CAN PUT MY WHOLE FOOT IN MY MOUTH!

YOU'RE GROSS!

The WORST NIGHTMARE
you ever had

Rules for your

1. Don't talk to me before 8:00 in the morning.

2. Don't make me sit next to my little brother on spaghetti night.

3. Don't walk into my room without knocking first.

4. Don't borrow my underwear under any circumstances.

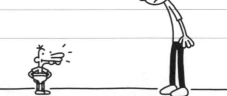

FAMILY

1.

2.

3.

4.

Your life, by

Longest you've ever
gone without bathing:

_____

Most bowls of cereal you've
ever eaten at one time:

_____

Longest you've ever been grounded: _____

Latest you've ever
been for school:

_____

Number of times you've
been chased by a dog:

_____

Number of times you've been
locked out of the house:

_____

 the numbers

Most hours you've spent
doing homework in one night:

_____

Most money you've ever saved up: _____

 Length of the shortest book
you've ever used for a book report:

_____

Farthest distance you've ever walked:

_____

Longest you've ever gone without watching TV:

 _____

Number of times   Number of times you've
you've gotten caught   gotten away with
picking your nose: picking your nose:

_____   _____

Unfinished

Li'l Cutie

" *Mommy, did my pencil go to heaven?* "

Li'l Cutie

"

COMICS

Li'l Cutie

Li'l Cutie

Make your

"   "

OWN comics

The FIRST FOUR LAWS you'll pass when you get elected president

1.

2.

3.

4.

" I hereby decree that no middle school student shalt have to take a shower after Phys Ed. "

The BADDEST THING
you ever did as a little kid

Practice your
SIGNATURE

You'll be famous one day, so let's face it...that signature of yours is gonna need some work. Use this page to practice your fancy new autograph.

List your INJURIES

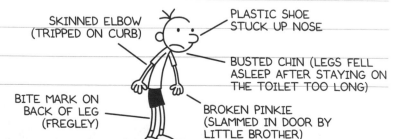

SKINNED ELBOW
(TRIPPED ON CURB)

PLASTIC SHOE
STUCK UP NOSE

BUSTED CHIN (LEGS FELL
ASLEEP AFTER STAYING ON
THE TOILET TOO LONG)

BITE MARK ON
BACK OF LEG
(FREGLEY)

BROKEN PINKIE
(SLAMMED IN DOOR BY
LITTLE BROTHER)

A few questions

Do you believe in unicorns?

If you ever got to meet a unicorn, what would you ask it?

Have you ever drawn a picture that was so scary that it gave you nightmares?

How many nights a week do you sleep in your parents' bed?

from ROWLEY

Have you ever tied your shoes without help from a grown-up?

Have you ever gotten sick from eating cherry lip gloss?

Are your friends jealous that you're a really good skipper?

The BIGGEST MISTAKES

1. Believing my older brother when he said it was "Pajama Day" at my school.

2. Taking a dare that probably wasn't worth it.

3. Giving Timmy Brewer my empty soda bottle.

you've made so far

1.

2.

3.

Unfinished

Creighton the Cretin

COMICS

Creighton the Cretin

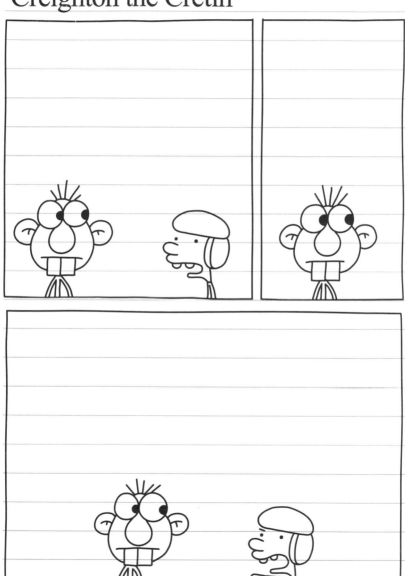

Make your

OWN comics

RODRICK'S

INTELLIGENCE TESTER:

Do this maze and then check to see if you're dumb or smart.

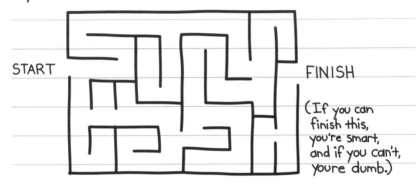

START   FINISH

(If you can finish this, you're smart, and if you can't, you're dumb.)

Put this sentence up to a mirror and then read it as loud as you can:

I AM A MORON.

Fill in the blank below:

Q: Who is awesome?

A: RODR_CK

(Hint: "I")

ACTIVITY PAGES

Answer this question yes or no <u>only</u>:

Q: Are you embarrassed that you pooped in your diaper today?

_____

Do you want to start a band? Well I guess you're out of luck because the best name is already taken and that's Löded Diper. But if you still want to start a band then you can use this mix-and-match thing: *

FIRST HALF	SECOND HALF
Wikkid	Lizzerd
Nästy	Pigz
Vilent	Vömmit
Rabbid	Dagger
Killer	Syckle
Ransid	Smellz

* P.S. If you use one of these names you owe me a hundred bucks.

# How well do you

Answer these questions, and then ask your friend the same things. Keep track of how many answers you got right.

FRIEND'S NAME: _____

Has your friend ever gotten
carsick?   _____

If your friend could meet any
celebrity, who would it be?   _____

Where was your friend born?   _____

Has your friend ever laughed
so hard that milk came out
of their nose?   _____

Has your friend ever been
sent to the principal's office?   _____

9–10: YOU KNOW YOUR FRIEND SO WELL IT'S SCARY
6–8: NOT BAD...YOU KNOW YOUR FRIEND PRETTY WELL!

know your FRIEND?

What's your friend's favorite
junk food?

_____

Has your friend ever broken
a bone?

_____

When was the last time your
friend wet the bed?

_____

If your friend had to
permanently transform into
an animal, what animal would
it be?

_____

Is your friend secretly
afraid of clowns?

_____

Now count up your correct answers and look at the
scale below to see how you did.

2–5: DID YOU GUYS JUST MEET OR SOMETHING?
0–1: TIME TO GET A NEW FRIEND

If you had a

If you could go back in time and change the future, but you only had five minutes, where would you go?

If you could go back in time and witness any event in history, what would it be?

If you had to be stuck living in some time period in the past, what time period would you pick?

TIME MACHINE...

If you could go back and videotape one event from your own life, what would it be?

If you could go back and tell your past self one thing, what would it be?

If you could go forward in time and tell your future self something, what would it be?

Totally awesome

The "Stand on One Foot" trick

STEP ONE: On your way home from school, bet your friend they can't stand on one foot for three minutes without talking.

STEP TWO: While your friend stands on one foot, knock real hard on some crabby neighbor's front door.

STEP THREE: Run.

PRACTICAL JOKES

A JOKE YOU'VE PLAYED ON A FRIEND:

A JOKE YOU'VE PLAYED ON A FAMILY MEMBER:

A JOKE YOU'VE PLAYED ON A TEACHER:

Your DRESSING

If you end up being a famous musician or a movie star, you're gonna need to put together a list of things you'll need in your dressing room.

Requirements for Greg Heffley - page 1 of 9

3 liters of grape soda

2 extra-large pepperoni pizzas

2 dozen freshly baked chocolate chip cookies

1 bowl of jelly beans (no pink or white ones)

1 popcorn machine

1 52-inch plasma TV

3 video game consoles with 10 games apiece

1 soft-serve ice cream machine

10 waffle cones

1 terry-cloth robe

1 pair of slippers

*** bathroom must have heated toilet seat

*** toilet paper must be name brand

ROOM requirements

You might as well get your list together now so that you're ready when you hit the big time.

Unfinished

The Amazing Fart Police

COMICS

The Amazing Fart Police

Make your

OWN comics

You, best ideas fur

BAD-BREATH DEFLECTOR

ELECTRIC FAN

HEAVY-DUTY ELASTIC STRAP

MR. HHHHHEFFLEY, DO YOU HHHHAVE YOUR HHHHOMEWORK?

WHIRR

ANIMAL TRANSLATOR

HEADSET

COMPUTER PACK

MICRO-PHONE

BARK! BARK! BARK!

HELLO! HELLO! HELLO!

FLAVOR STICK

ROLLING PIN COATED WITH POTATO CHIP FLAVOR DUST

(FLAVOR DUST CAN BE SOUR CREAM AND ONION, CHEDDAR CHEESE, OR BARBECUE)

LICK

INVENTIONS

WRITE DOWN YOUR OWN AWESOME IDEAS
SO YOU CAN PROVE YOU CAME UP WITH
THEM BEFORE ANYONE ELSE.

Make a map of your

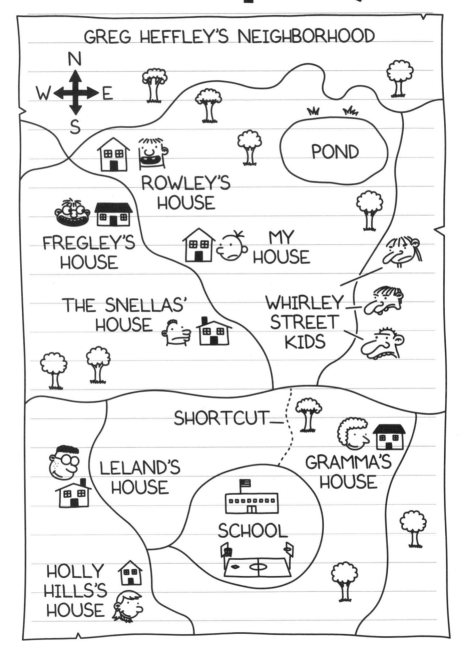

GREG HEFFLEY'S NEIGHBORHOOD

N
W E
S

ROWLEY'S HOUSE

POND

FREGLEY'S HOUSE

MY HOUSE

THE SNELLAS' HOUSE

WHIRLEY STREET KIDS

SHORTCUT

LELAND'S HOUSE

GRAMMA'S HOUSE

SCHOOL

HOLLY HILLS'S HOUSE

NEIGHBORHOOD

YOUR NEIGHBORHOOD

¡Make your own...

FRONT

Dear Aunt Jean,
THANK YOU
for the wonderful socks
you knitted for me.

INSIDE

But next time, could we
just stick with cash?

DORK!

SHOVE

FRONT

I'm sorry
that it didn't work out
with you and Lyndsey.

INSIDE

P.S. Could you
find out if she
thinks I'm "cute"?

GREETING CARDS

FRONT

INSIDE

FRONT

INSIDE

The BEST VACATION
you ever went on

Make a Löded Diper CONCERT POSTER

Unfinished

Xtreme Sk8ers

THE END

COMICS

Xtreme Sk8ers

THE END

Make your

If you had

If you had the power to read other people's thoughts, would you really want to use it?

YES ☐   NO ☐

If you were a super hero, would you want to have a sidekick?   YES ☐   NO ☐

SUPERPOWERS...

If you were a super hero, would you keep your identity secret?   YES ☐   NO ☐

Would you want to have X-ray vision if you couldn't turn it off?   YES ☐   NO ☐

Draw your FRIENDS

the way Greg Heffley would

A few questions

Do you ever put food in your belly button so you can have a snack later on?

Do animals ever use their thoughts to talk to you?

Has your guidance counselor ever called you "unpredictable and dangerous"?

from FREGLEY

If you had a tail, what would you do with it?

Have you ever eaten a scab?

Do you wanna play "Diaper Whip"?

Have you ever been sent home from school early for "hygiene issues"?

> You probably didn't wipe good enough again, Fregley.

Autographs

GET YOUR FRIENDS
TO WRITE STUFF
IN THIS BOOK.

Autographs

Create your own COVER

DIARY
of a

What's YOUR story?

Use the rest of this book to keep a daily journal, write a novel, draw comic strips, or tell your life story.

But whatever you do, make sure you put this book someplace safe after you finish it.

Because when you're rich and famous, this thing is gonna be worth a FORTUNE.

ABOUT THE AUTHOR

(THAT'S YOU)

ACKNOWLEDGMENTS

(THE PEOPLE YOU WANT TO THANK)